BETWEEN DRYDEN
ANOTHER COLLEC

BETWEEN DRYDEN AND DUFFY: ANOTHER COLLECTION

ANN DRYSDALE

With thanks
for an inspiring
speech

Ann Drysdale

"ACORN" – 21.10.5.

First published in 2005 by Peterloo Poets
The Old Chapel, Sand Lane, Calstock,
Cornwall PL18 9QX, U.K.

**A catalogue record for this book is available
from the British Library
ISBN 1-904324-29-0**

Front cover illustration: Beryl Cook. *Dustbinmen,*
from *Private View* (John Murray Ltd., 1980)
© Beryl Cook 1980 (reproduced by arrangement
with the artist c/o Rogers, Coleridge & White Ltd.)

Printed in Great Britain by
Antony Rowe Ltd, Chippenham, Wilts.

ACKNOWLEDGEMENTS

Thanks are due to the editors of *Acumen, Connections,* and *Equinox,* in which several of the poems in this volume first appeared. "Perfect Binding" was included in the *World Book Day Anthology* (Stonebridge)

"Mallard" was a prizewinner in the 2003 Bridport Competition. "Running through Dandelions" and "Goose, Gone" were prizewinners in the 2003 and 2004 Peterloo competitions. "Forgive Me If I Don't Get Up" and "My Lover Bought Me Saffron" were runners-up in Poetry on the Lake 2004, and "Among Roses" took third prize in the 2004 Wells Festival Competition.

"A Landscape in Waiting" was commissioned by Bargoed Town Council, supported by Academi and Cydcoed, to celebrate the creation of a woodland park. The resultant publication, illustrated by photographer Tim Collier, was nominated for Welsh Book of the Year.

tibi: namque tu solebas
meas esse aliquid putare nugas.

Catullus: *Poem number 1*

CONTENTS

Running Through Dandelions

A field of stubble; all the grain is gone,
The straw is baled and led, the headland bare
Unless you count the weeds that carry on
From now till ploughing. Look! A springing hare
Goes thumping through the soft midsummer dust.
His forepaws tap the ground; with muscled might
His hind legs overtake and flex and thrust
And throw him forward in ecstatic flight –
Lubb-dupp. As though his heart were in his feet
He gallops in exaggerated mime,
His tireless iambs counting out the beat
That underpins the dandelion time.
Rehearsing joy, anticipating fear,
He dances for the turning of the year.

And So – for Steven

A kid's funeral on the news. Cameras pan
long rows of school friends' flowers and cards ...

From *So* by Steven Blyth

"We will always love you *(so)* very much".
Adult amendment to a child's regret.
It looks like an unnecessary touch;
I wonder if you've seen a reason yet?
When human beings have to handle grief
They often show such touching innocence,
Holding on tight to the forlorn belief
That how you write things makes a difference.
So – hold your children. Shield them while you can
From the sad fact the nameless stranger knew;
That there are times when nothing else will scan
And only a pentameter will do.

From "A Landscape in Waiting"

1. Re-configuring Lowry

Looking again at the scene L.S.Lowry painted – Bargoed 1965

It was as if someone had taken a spoon to Mount Fuji
And cracked it and scooped off the top of it like a boiled egg.
Someone had taken a rubber to Lowry's tall chimneys
And blown away all the detritus along with the smoke.
No towering spoil heap, no industry – so much has vanished;
Only the viaduct, houses and river remain.

A canvas scraped clean of its former formidable darkness;
A landscape in waiting to see what the world will do next.

But soon firm hands will impaste a new highway across it
To lead the eye outward towards the rest of the world
While others will slyly apply all their skills to the
                        background
Changing a bit at a time the sad grey into green
And here and there we will plug in small blobs of bright
                        colour
And smudge them softly into the chiaroscuro
And then we will seek out the smallest, the finest of brushes
And carefully put in the people that Lowry forgot.

2. For Idris Davies

Oh, can you see the Rhymney now
From where your face is hid?
And can you see the things we've done
To mend the things we did?

There's otters on the river now
Where pools are clear and deep
And ten yards up from Gilfach bridge
I saw a salmon leap.

Soon lucky folk will walk to work
Through seasons' changing faces
And valley boys will court and spark
In green secluded places.

Where once there grew a common greed
For iron and for coal
We recognise a deeper need
In matters of the soul.

We are trying, Idris, trying
To help the dream along:
A people fit for poetry;
A river fit for song.

(Deleted stanzas ...)

But the factories at Britannia
Are still disgorging foam
And Valley boys don't think it's cool
To take their litter home,

So silver poison now and then
Goes floating up above
And underfoot the seeds and skins
Betray the fruits of love.

3. Nobody's Ground

Alongside one of the gates into Paradise
There stands a burnt-out car. I asked a bloke,
Rhetorically,
Why anyone would do a thing like that.
Why not? he said. *What's it to do with you.*
It's not your ground – it's nobody's ground, innit?

He was a big chap and I was too scared
To answer him. But after he had gone
I called him up in spirit; put my point,
Brave as could be. *Nobody's ground?*
What do you mean by that, then – nobody's ground?

Is it so difficult to comprehend?
Roll it round in your head a bit, my friend.
See what you make of it.
It's nobody's ground if it isn't somebody's ground
Which means it could be anybody's ground
So, by extension, everybody's ground.
That gives you rights all right, sunshine.
But what about responsibility?

Oh, I was brave, in the absence of challenge.
I knew exactly what to say and said it.
Another day I'll tell him to his face.

But meanwhile, who will remove the car?
Who will remove the car?

4. "Leaves of Grass"

"Grass don't have leaves," said Rhys, emphatically,
Scratching his fashionable Number One.
"Why not?" I asked, hoping to lead the child
Into an edifying conversation.
"Cos it's grass, innit" said Rhys. "End of story."

Rhys is a city kid; grass is an outdoor carpet,
An early prototype of Astroturf.
It is not even stuff; it is a thing
That does your head in, always wanting cutting.
He has been born unto the generation
That coined the verb "to patio".

Like the close relative who hits a child
Repeatedly, giving the flawed reason
That it is for the youngster's benefit,
These good citizens castigate their grass,
Saying "it wanted doing".

Rhys can no more conceive of leaves of grass
Than can his little shaven bullet-head
Admit the possibility of ringlets.

"But if you left it alone," I confided
"It would grow leaves for you, high as your head."
With a swift gesture that implied a word
That he was still too young to understand
He dismissed the implausible notion.

I pointed to the hills above his house –
"One day," I said (having read the Urban Plan)
"There will be trees up there for you to play in
And grass that no-one cuts." But he was gone,
A swift image of an incontinent puppy,
One short leg impelling his bright scooter.

It is a leap of faith for both of us;
Rhys's small bald head isn't ready yet
To explore the gorgeous possibility
And I, old cynic, only just believe
That trees will grow on all that desolation
And young Rhys may one day lie with a lover
Among the leaves of grass.

5. Mallard

Beady-eyed wide-boy, cheerful polymath
Who's never quite as good at anything
As anybody else. Oh, he can fly
But not as the swift flies, not as the kestrel.
He gets there, though, after his own fashion,
And he can swim, but not as the swan swims.
Even his scavenging is overshadowed
By that of gulls, his small predations by
The lordly heron. His are little skills
Thoughtlessly exhibited ad infinitum
In his own idiosyncratic world.
I asked him once, "Mallard, my feathered friend,
What do you do, exactly? What are you *for*?"
His reply was a wink and a wet shrug;
"Oh, you know, Squire – bit of this, bit of that;
Bit of ducking and diving. Grab what's going.
Know what I mean, Squire, eh? Know what I mean?"

6. Sand Martins on the Rhymney

Swift-scooting along the gentle curve of the river,
Panicking sand martins, newly arrived from wherever,
Are looking out for short-term accommodation.
Bat-flittering hopefully against the retaining wall,
They peer into the open ends of drainage pipes –
"Hello-o! Anybody ho-ome?"

Our gullible ancestors used to believe that the swallows
Who dipped in long swoops to kiss the surface of water
Would, at the first sign of summer's ending,
Dive deep to lie warm in the comforting mud until spring.

For they do sound a bit far-fetched, these tales of migration,
And standing here leaning on railings beside the Rhymney
I could convince myself without very much trouble
That the martins have dribbled forth from the ends of the
                                        drainpipes,
Sucked out by the sunshine.

7. Seascape, with Waders

People planting trees. The sound of laughter
Ripples like tinsel through the scattered group.
Some backs are bent, others straighten and turn
Then dip and lift the whips one at a time.
Some strike their spades against the ground, then pause,
Then stamp and push and lift again and turn.
Men, women, children in a common dance,
All movement, stretching away up the hill.

And now, as I stand back a moment, watching,
Wind blurs my eyes. I blink. And find myself
Back on a windswept beach somewhere in Norfolk
Where stilty birds are toddling, heads down,
Each within reach of a like-minded individual,
All utterly at home in their own space
Doing whatever they do, in fits and starts,
Twittering happily in a common purpose.

8. Japanese Knotweed

The enemy is at the gate.
Spear-points are already visible in the wood.
Their numbers are unimaginable and Oh,
What must we do to be saved?

Our horticultural forebears,
Seeking a quick fix for awkward corners,
Sowed dragon's teeth and now the whole land
Is reaping the consequences.

First scarlet dwarves appear
One, two, a hundred – soon tall halberdiers
Line up in Lincoln green, young and defiant.
Snap one and two will grow.

Then verdant cavalry gather,
White plumes nodding above their heads,
Dropping confetti onto spreading capes,
And emerald caparisons.

And now, though only spear-points
Are visible above the shattered debris
Of last year's battle, it begins again and Oh,
What can we do to be saved?

9. Colonisation

In the park, in the old part – the deep green-and-gold part
Where trees long established compete for the sky,
The pines and the beeches, extending their reaches,
Are holding a canopy heavenly-high.

All long-ago planted and taken for granted
They furnish fine sites for discreet little homes
With bird-nesting-boxes and ditches for foxes
And bolt-holes for badgers and niches for gnomes.

Wild things are nesting here, working and resting here.
Come very carefully; move like a mouse
For beneath the old beech where the world cannot reach
A remarkable creature is building a house.

Discreet as can be with no harm to the tree
It has fashioned in secret a place of its own –
A den where a child can be happy and wild
And be wholly itself and entirely alone.

It is hard to believe what a child can achieve
Given space to imagine and freedom to act.
It has found what it needed – and we have succeeded,
For this is the species we hoped to attract.

10. Dogs in their Private Progress

See the solitary dogs in the park
They have come here on their own for a lark
They are to-ing, they are fro-ing
And there is no way of knowing
Where they've been or where they're going
Through the park

See the busy little dogs in the park
Greet each other with a brisk little bark
Watch their tiny teeth a-snapping
See their jaunty tails a-flapping
Hear their merry toenails tapping
Through the park

See the dating, mating dogs in the park
As they stop and lift their legs to make their mark
They are sniffing, they are smelling
Their relationships are gelling
Hear their owners' far-off yelling
Through the park

Secret dogs come out at night in the park
Take a torch and see their eyes in the dark
They are gleaming and unblinking
And you can't tell what they're thinking
When the midnight dogs go slinking
Through the park

11. Ends and Beginnings

In the old wood, high on the hill, a beech tree is dying.
Roots like old hands clinging hard to the side of the slope.
A cause for respect and regret; a source of sadness.
A time for saying goodbye and for letting go.
When the children come here to plant primroses and violets
Let us tell them about the old tree and the fact of its going.
Let us teach them the truth about change, let us show them a
                                                    future,
Otherwise all they will have is a sense of bereavement,
A constant need to keep saying sorry, sorry,
Crystallised in a theme park.

12. The Little Beaches

When the Rhymney is not in spate, there are little beaches
Where you can step down onto a shingle spar
And stand listening to the singing of the river
As it spins along under the dripping cliffs.
But when your eye tires of the tiny waterfalls
And the random tufting of perfect little ferns
You should look down to see what lies at your feet.
Here is all manner of undervalued treasure:
Neck of an old stone bottle; a round mouth
Puckered to suck in liquor; piece of green glass
Tumbled from a weapon into a gentle jewel.
Here is a rose-red, all-but-spherical pebble –
O river, anorak, nerd, what on earth are you up to?
You, who could cool iron, wash coal and drown children,
Have you no sense of history, time or propriety
That you settle for making a small ball out of a brick?

13. Ethnic Cleansing

They are strung out along the dusty road,
The wiry peasants who have long subsisted
On what this grim place had to offer them.
Small, feisty alders, with their tight blue buds
Like chilblained knuckles of uncherished children;
Brave buddleias, standing beside the highway
With their cheap scent and unsubtle colours,
Winking at passers-by, hoping for love.
Someone has sprayed them with a blaze of orange
And it is only a matter of time.
But they stand with their buds breaking, bearing
Enforced insignia of the undesirable,
Waiting for the two-stroke cough of the chain-saw
As it sets about its business – *rrrrraus!, rrrrraus!, rrrrraus!*

14. Giving it Away

Official opening of the park – 9th July 2003

High on the hill, I stood watching the carnival marchers
Coming from all the four corners of what I surveyed.
I felt as if soldiers were coming to capture my castle
And I was alone, undefended, in tears and afraid.

Animal masks, painted faces and war-drums and banners;
Signs of the Ostrogoth, Saxon and Chartist and change.
All that was mine would belong from now on to all comers
And all the beloved familiar would now become strange.

I gathered a flower, just one of the thousands around me.
Knapweed. I twisted its stalk round its neck and pulled tight
And then with a tweak I let fly at the foes that opposed me.
The purple head fell at my feet without gathering flight.

"Missed!" cried a voice from my past. "That was bloody
                                        pathetic!"
And the ghost of a plantain bud whistled an inch from my ear
As the friend who had taught me the aerodynamics of flowers
Came into my head to remind of why I was here.

It was places like this that created my feeling for nature;
It was deep in long grass that my singular selfhood was
                                        found
And all that I am I can trace to the time that I wasted
In childhood, in secret, in dangerous play on rough ground.

For the wildness and wilderness has to exist for a reason
And it would be foolish to keep the invaders at bay
For the cohorts are marching towards me to take it and keep it
And now, to ensure it survives, I must give it away.

15. Wrong Tongue?

By the waters of Rhymney I sat down
And wept when I remembered the fierce joy
Of first setting foot in this special place.

I was your bard, Rhymney, chosen and crowned;
Chosen to sing the songs the place gave me,
Crowned with the echo and chime of my finding.

But they that paid my wages wanted more,
Calling for one last song from me, saying
Now then, poet: *Canwch gân yn Gymraeg!*

Alas, I do not have the gift of Welsh.
I have sung faithfully in my own voice
Because it is all I have to offer.

Oh, Rhymney, Rhymney, tell me, is it true?
Have I been singing your song all along
In the wrong tongue?

Between Dryden and Duffy

That's where I look in every one of them –
Ottakar's, Hammick's, Hatchard's, Waterstone's.
Finding my books displayed in none of them
Do I descend to star-defeated moans?
Not I! With an assumed shortsighted stoop on,
I check the coast is clear to right and left.
Then, with a Waitrose bag held slightly open
As if in readiness for petty theft,
I make my hand into a living axe
Which parts the volumes at a single stroke.
Then, with my fingers, I enlarge the cracks
And *slip one in*, like an unscripted joke.
Booksellers do not view this with delight;
It wrecks their paperwork. And serves them right.

An Alternative Proposal

To be sung to the tune *Aurelia* (The Church's One Foundation)

Each daily dump is vital
Each tiny tinkle's great
More power for the people
Each job will generate.
When droppings are donated
Each loyal Welshman smiles.
If you are constipated
Then God will give you piles.

The spirit of the Chartists
Shall not cry out in vain
For Cambrian piss-artists
Will strike the porcelain
And all along our plumbing
From todger, twat and tush
The power will be humming
With every mighty flush.

We shall not be affrighted
When Britain's blackout comes;
We shall not be benighted
While Welshmen still have bums.
For we will eat jalfrezi
In bold Glendower's name
And then we'll crap like crazy
And light the lamps again.

O, hear Rebecca's daughter
Proclaim these fighting words:
The *sais* have seized our water;
They shall not take our turds!
When there's no windy weather
And fossil fuel fails,
Then we will squat together
And we will shit for Wales!

The Independent Wales Party opposed the construction of a windfarm on Coity Mountain, claiming that it would benefit England more than Wales. They proposed instead that a people's co-operative should take over the sewers, and that effluent from the community should run down a series of steep steps so as to generate electricity on its way to the sea. However, they failed to explain the trigonometry...

Risk Assessment

*Written at the request of Blaenau Gwent Council prior to
a series of poetry workshops in Bryn Bach Park. 20.6.04*

The whole enterprise is fraught with hazard
When you come to think about it. No parent
Would ever let their child participate
Knowing the full extent of the danger.
Huddled for an hour in a sweaty tent
With only a poet to take care of them?
They could be inappropriately touched,
Approached by some ungodly reprobate
Offering to show them skylarks in return
For a quick peep at their budding talent.
They might catch fire; rub two ideas together
And – *poof!* – spontaneous creativity!
Addiction is a possibility
And the susceptible may find themselves
Unable to resist the strong compulsion
To indulge repeatedly in the habit,
For, as the wise poet wrote on the packet,
This stuff can seriously affect the heart.*

*paraphrasing Elma Mitchell's *This Poem* ...

Teaching in the Forest

1. Bluebells

Walking in single file,
carefully, carefully –
don't squash the bluebells with
hurrying feet.
Go to the edge of them
thoughtfully, thoughtfully.
Stand very still where the
two colours meet.
Green of the forest and
blue of the meadow. But
who can compare them and
what are they worth?
Stand very quietly.
Savour the silence of
blueness and greenness and
Heaven and Earth.

2. Running Wild

In a clearing surrounded by trees
Children are running wild –
Shrill yells and handbrake turns,
Loud howls and stuntman falls.
We have talked about nuts and acorns
We have sung about birds and squirrels
And now to reward their diligence
We have set them free to celebrate
The otherness of outdoors.
They are running around at random
Till they fall in small heaps, laughing
And drumming their heels on the carpet
That nature unrolled underneath them
Till their knees and elbows are covered
With new-mown green shag-pile.

Don't move the cooker!

This darksome cranny, dogshit brown
With dingy dollops dribbling down,
Where the last of the toast and the rest of the roast
Do lie beyond eye in the heart of the host.

Where there hangs and dangles the mélange among,
Like the grim little ghost of a guinea-pig's tongue,
A sharp-shrivelled shaving of Parma ham
O'er the pitchblack puddle that might have been jam.

The curled-up crust and the long-lost cloth
And the paper-thin skin of the boiled-over broth
They lie as they fell and they sleep there yet
In their breath-blown bedding of gossamer net.

Oh, where would the world be, once bereft
Of gunge and of ghastliness. Let them be left,
O let them be left, leave them in peace;
The breadcrumbs, the dead crumbs, the God-given grease.

For My Sister, at Fifty

There were three twigs on a family tree,
nine, eleven and twenty-one;
one was you and one was me,
the other a brother whose tale is done.
Nine, eleven and twenty-one,
the numbers were odd and so were they.
Twenty-one subtracted herself,
married a waster and ran away.
And when eleven was twenty-three,
twice himself and a year to spare,
he died on a road in a far country
and we cancelled him out and left him there.
Each original multiplied
leaving remainders, three, two, one,
the laws of progression satisfied
by the several sequences thus begun.
Now the numbers are even again,
half-a-hundred and sixty two,
and I love you now as I loved you then.
This is my birthday gift for you.

Chinoiserie

Théophile Gautier

I am in love, although you're not the one
I love. It is not Juliet I prize,
Ophelia or Beatrice or even
The lovely Laura with her big soft eyes.

My latest love is living in Cathay
Devoted to her aged parents, far
Up in a tower of brittle porcelain
By the Yellow River where the cormorants are.

Her eyes are tilted slits, her little foot
Would fit into my hand, her complexion
Is like the parchment of a lampshade, lit
From within. Her nails are red and long.

She leans her head over her balcony;
The passing swallows dip to touch her hair
As every night she sings, and poetry
Spins willow and peach-blossom in the air.

During the Storm

Théophile Gautier

The boat is a speck in a thundering ocean,
The waves toss us up to a mutinous sky
Which drops us back down to the water's commotion
And here, where the mast was, we kneel and we pray.

There's only a plank between us and forever
And maybe tonight we shall all lie asleep
In a bitter black bed with a white frothy cover,
Lamplit by lightning and lost in the deep.

Saviour of sailors in danger of dying,
Our own Blessed Lady, the Flower of Heaven,
Calm the waves' clamour and hush the wind's crying
And push with your finger our boat into haven.

And if you will save us we promise we'll give you
A really big candle with fancy bits on;
We'll get you a gown made of glittery tissue
And carve, for your Jesus, a little Saint John.

Hippopotamus

Théophile Gautier

Gargantuan-gutted Hippo sits
At home in Java's jungly bits,
Where mutter in each dark recess
More monsters than a man can guess.

Constrictors hiss as they uncoil,
Tiger performs his horrid howl,
Buffalo snorts in search of strife
But Hippo just gets on with life.

He's not afraid of sword or spear;
He stands his ground when man is near.
The natives' grapeshot makes him grin
By bouncing off his leather skin.

And I'm just like the hippo, me.
Protected by complacency.
Armed cap-à-pie with what I know,
Through the wild world unfazed I go.

After Verlaine

1. The Blaina Gnome

Down by the bowling-green the mooning gnome
Winks over his shoulder at his own arse
As if to tell us that no good will come
From these enchanted moments. They will pass;
The secret you and I came here to find –
Two solemn pilgrims following our stars –
Already being driven out of mind
By the rude music blaring from parked cars.

2. Verlaine at 5am

It's raining out there and here in my head.
Looks a bit dismal; feel a bit dead.
Going's unstable; watch where you tread.
Tomorrow? Tomorrow. 'Nuff said, 'nuff said.

Oh Dear Me – Did The Little Birdie Die, Then?

Catullus. Poem Number 3

Cry your eyes out, love-goddesses and godlings
(And all men with anthropomorphic leanings).
My bird's bird's been and gone and turned its toes up.
Bird, that is, that my own bird used to fancy,
Bird she loved even better than her eyeballs.
Sickly-sweet bird. Disgustingly familiar;
Used to act like a baby with its mother,
Squat her crotch or canoodle in her bosom,
Always flitting from one place to the other,
Chirping things she pretended to make sense of.
Now it's gone down the long and shady alley
"From whose bourne no traveller returns," like.
Shame on you, oh you naughty Powers of Darkness!
Old Grim Reaper, who gobbles all the goodies,
Bagged a bird of particular importance.
Oh, dear me! Poor old Tweetie! What a bummer!
It's your fault that my little love is blubbing
And her eyes are all pinky-rimmed and puffy.

*This translation did not find favour with the classical scholar who judged
the competition in which I entered it. He called me a "naughty boy".
However, it is founded on the assumption (based on the poem which precedes
it) that, despite how "Lesbia" may have felt about the bird, Catullus himself
was not displeased to see the back of it. Perhaps he throttled it.*

One-off

Catullus. Poem number 32

Students, here is a problematic poem;
Odd one out in the canon of Catullus . . .

I will love you, beloved Ipsitilla
If you make me a window in your schedule –
After lunch would be first among my druthers.
Please be there; I would really love to see you.
Don't lock up; I'm in something of a hurry –
Norwich, my darling – if you get my meaning!
Give you one? Give you nine if you're a good girl!
Stuffed with food, I am in the mood for stuffing;
Say the word and I'll come around and show you
How my prick has arisen for the business,
Mister Stiff, who is poking through my clothing.

The Love-song of Ipsitilla

Oh, Mr Catullus, I love you so dearly
And yours is the name I cry out in the night
But you don't ever think of me, do you, not really?
I'm out of your mind when I'm out of your sight.
Yet when I am with you I find I can nearly
Believe you are truly my refuge and rock.
Alone I can see it remarkably clearly;
I only exist when I'm kissing your cock.
And when, on a whim, you decide to come to me
You slip me a wink as you walk in the yard
But when you're with her you look past me and through me;
It's terribly, terribly, terribly hard.
You call me and tell me you want to be with me,
You're feeling inspired and you need to confer;
You've something to show me and something to give me,
Your mind is on me but your heart is with her.
Yet Mr Catullus, although you abuse me,
In spite of the hurt and the hate and the pain
I know in my heart that however you use me
The next time you knock I will fuck you again.

For two thousand years scholars have guessed at the identity of the once-mentioned Ipsitilla, but poets have always known. She is simply "Ipsa et Illa"— that woman, and her song has been sung for centuries to the tune of a roistering jig.

Trevor's Way

I sit before my monitor;
Ensconced thereon is my cat, Trevor.
What is he sitting on it for?
Solidarity Forever!

Here I practise poetry,
The art that dares not speak its name.
I watch for incongruity;
Trevor's doing much the same.

I creep from one page to the next
Ever anxious to determine
Infelicities of text;
Trevor watches out for vermin.

I will grab a passing thought
In my unselective net,
Fiddle with the thing I've caught,
Wonder if I've killed it yet.

"Yeah!" says Trevor, "that's the 'ammer!
Get it down and do it rough;
Save the scansion and the grammar
Till you're sure it's pukka stuff."

That's how Trevor treats his prey,
Elegant exterminator!
Eats the innards straight away;
Saves the little feet till later.

Based on an 9th century jeu d'esprit, written in Irish by an anonymous monk on a Latin manuscript found in a monastery in Austria.

Old Cat Asleep

Mim dozes wheezily on the windowsill,
Tongue a protruding tube, discoloured teeth
Pinning her muzzle into a fixed picture
Of sour disapproval.
A column of cold drool connects her scowl
To her uneasy feet, which grope and grip,
Wielding unnecessary needles.

Unloveliness is overlooked; I love her.
Love? Love: I have known her a long time;
Brought her from house to house, a living link
With all that muddled past.
She has put up with times of little care,
Amused herself with the production of
A few indifferent kittens.

Apparently peripheral, although
She has affected several decisions
As resident responsibility,
Part of the flow one goes with; who can tell
How great has been her influence?

She fritters hours, eyes closed, pulling and pricking;
Unpicking petit point,
Industriously kneading the idea of bread,
Busy feet treading the slow mills of God,
Squeezing small grapes of wrath.

Mending a Snail

Some anonymous bird made a fine mess of your shell;
You were slithering on, broken, perhaps to your death.

I saw you on the road because my eyes were downcast,
Me thinking strange and lugubrious thoughts at the time.

My beloved is dead; he who so loved to mend things;
Whom I was unable to mend when push came to shove.

Sutures and surgical tape could not hold him together
And neither could love. I tried and I failed and he died.

Holding what's left of you, I assess the damage. Triage.
Save you or put a swift end to your life with a brick?

Unusual way to look at a snail; through your roof
At your working parts throbbing under a thin, clear skin

Like my love's belly after the botched operation.
Peristalsis. The proverbial way to his heart.

With leftover dressings I practise old skills on you;
Découpage. Papier mâché. Bookbinding, even.

As I work you bend and watch, touching my fingernails
With your sniffing eyes, sticking your damp foot to my hand.

Whole again, little one, in a manner of speaking.
Bodged, jury-rigged, you are now my beloved concern.

I will give you a bottle-garden, your own Eden.
I will bring food to you, and friends, and play God for you.

Through the glass I admire your exquisite underneath;
A kiss in aspic, a flat heart with a hole in it.

Dogs in the Wind

Facing four-square into the roaring West,
The little mongrel bravely stands his ground
Among the tempest-tattered meadow-grass.
His hair combed back by the wind's strong fingers,
He holds tight to the earth with spiny feet
As panic-stricken things go whirling past,
Riding on yellow leaves.

Hearing another unfamiliar sound,
Regular thumping of a tuned machine,
He turns, tickled by curiosity.
The wind has blown the dust off a lost cause
And the old lurcher, high on borrowed time,
Ears thin as string, mouth wide, cheeks wuthering,
Remembers how to fly.

Goose, gone

Cissie the goose is gone.
Down to the water they go,
Her lovely footprints, ivy leaves in snow.
The pond is frozen but old Cissie
Probably doesn't know.

Old goose, old friend. Bless her,
I shall go down and break the ice for her,
Take the hard lid off the water
That she has gone down for.

Oh no!
There she lies in the snow,
Her neck stretched and her eyes taken.
The fox has been. See how his sharp teeth tore
Her stout heart from her poor breast
Before he lost interest.

A little blood, a few feathers;
Spilt, pulled. Wasted.
He can scarcely have tasted
Her dark flesh.

If he had only dragged her home,
Her breast against his knees, banging
And her fine head hanging low,
Taking her back to feed his family –
But no.

Cissie the goose is gone, and Oh,
How shall I tell the children?

Here I stand

Ich kann nicht anders...

I am a bunny rabbit and
No grass than mine is greener
Though hares are better looking and
Considerably leaner;
A hare has more charisma and
A hare has greater grace
But I'm a bunny rabbit with a
Bunny-rabbit face.
A rabbit's what I look like
And a rabbit's what I go like,
And what you see is what you get –
That's all ye need to know, like.

High Tide

A spring tide on the Tamar
And all through the top of the afternoon
They were talking of it, planning
What they would do, where they would be, when it came.
Laughing and laying bets – *five pound says the top step* . . .

It's almost time. Boats knock and jostle.
Forces assemble, drifting towards the shore.
Bits, in all sizes ranging from lumps to dust,
Ride wearily home on the greasy skin of the river
And form themselves into a fidgeting queue at the step,
Awaiting repatriation.

And the natives wait, ready to leap into action,
Hoping and dreading and nobody giving a damn
Che sera sera!
Under the brave awning on the crowded quay
Glasses shimmer and chink.

A dog dives in from a boat,
Sending a shiver along the tethered line;
Drags himself out by the tips of his spiny fingers
Shaking himself into a fine shower of silver
That mimics the giggling of uneasy halyards.

A seagull, or perhaps a sandwich crust,
Bobs on the top of the tide,
Holding its own for a moment
Before the slowing flow gives way with a shrug
To the first quick suck of the sea.

And all of this at the arbitrary discretion
Of an indifferent moon.

Three from Crete

1. Outside Giorgio's

Cat dozes on a pile of fishing nets
Flexing his toes
Giving fives to the sunshine

Cloud fingers the edge of the mountain
Tickling the loose stones
Mimicking erosion

Something the cloud said
Casts a shadow
Threatens the sunshine

Cat makes fists

2. Sweetwater Beach

"We have a problem", said Muriel, carefully,
Shaking her head as she looked at the scenery.
Elderly man with his unfettered genitals
Picking his way over stones to the sea.

Far and away his most obvious attributes
Hanging like fruit in the shade of his corpulence
Perfectly formed, if a little degenerate,
Proudly proclaiming the magic of three.

3. Bright Fish

Beautiful tease,
sliding out from your rock into sunlight.
Green and gold;
scarlet and blue.
Purposeful as a slick torpedo
made of fallen rainbows.
Each day since I saw you
I have been back to the rock,
stood a while staring at weeds and lesser fishes.
No Show. Again and again, No Show.

Now, so afraid I didn't really see you,
I will go trawling for you in home waters –
Google. Britannica.
And Gunther Sterba's *Fishes of the World.*

I Saw Three Ships ...

Christmas on the canal.   Three narrowboats
Remain along the bank. Fair-weather folk
Have battened down their hatches and gone home.
Tracy is still here, though, pushing her luck –
Haphazard hippie, ragtag water-gypsy,
At loggerheads with the authorities.
They want her off because she hasn't got
The proper papers, but the other boaties
Regard her with affection. Up she comes
Out of the cabin with her tie-dyed tee-shirt
Under her chin, tattooed arms cherishing
The little boy who suckles at her breast.
A voice calls cheerfully across the cut,
Tits out for the lads then, is it, Tracy?
Eff-off! she yells, with equal lack of malice.

The Perkins coughs and catches, comes to life
With the slow pulsing of a steady heart.
Tracy sets off towards the water-point,
Steering with one hand as the lordly bow
Crumples the cat-ice in its gentle progress
And baby Jake, snuggled in grubby fleece,
Nests in the safe curve of her other arm.
He's fallen fast asleep. The rose-hip nipple
Lies in the loose curl of his petal tongue.
His lips mime kisses and one dimpled hand
Adorns the bare breast like a living star.

Queer Fish

For Jay

There he is in the corner,
Tom tiddler, in a pool of hands,
all reaching for him in liquid flickers; his mum, his girl,
quick fingers, slipping off his slick skin.
Others in pockets, unfeminine, flexing,
thinking the feel of Tom trout and
practising guddle and scoop.

Hi, Tom!

So much slighter than I had expected –
No wonder nobody's net holds him for long.
But he sits tall,
a lot of length between his head and haunches
and all of it shifting in ripples. A slim fish.
Tom stickleback, absorbing information
along his lateral line.

Karaoke!

All hips and shoulders, he makes for the microphone.
A different fish now; Tom smolt,
dipping and twisting
between the choking weedpeople,
diving to take the mike,
lifting it lovingly close enough to kiss,
punching up through the surface
with *The Power of Love.*

Where will he be, Tom salmon,
when the call comes?
Swimming upstream, probably,
against the flow.

Handling Sprats

Such wickedly delicious little fish
Curled stiff and brittle in their own crisp skins
Offering themselves to the soft fingers
That pick them diffidently from the dish.
Incinerated tiddlers. What to do?
Eyes meet. Conspire. Fortitude is called for.
No place for niceness now. Break off the head
And pull the chain of spine free from the flesh;
Manipulate the vulnerable meat
Into soft pellets to be dunked in sauce
That clings and tingles, red and sweet and hot.
Fish-fingers diving time and time again,
Each trip undertaken with more abandon.
Time to roll up the sleeves; the liquid drips
As far as wrists, threatening pristine cuffs.
A token gesture. After all, who cares?
Too soon two hands meet in an empty dish.
Time to wipe the last bits around the bowl,
Lick salty lips and suck the tips of digits.
Now eyes meet over the rims of smeared glasses
As temporarily besotted faces
Grin at each other over the remains
Of the miraculous draught of fishes.

Background Music

Ella sings "Is you is or is you ain't"
But now I know and need no longer guess.
You ain't. And now the soup is flavourless.

I talk too loudly. Ella sings again:
"you can't be mine and someone else's too"
Can't fault you, Miss Fitzgerald; this is true.

Ella is in her element. She sings
"Miss Otis regrets". Oh, Ella, so do I;
I'd give a lot not to have lunched today.

The fish is foul and the wine tastes of tar.
Ella is singing "all the things you are";
I cannot think of anything to say.

Ella sings "every time we say goodbye".
The sweetness leaches from the crème brulée.
I concentrate on trying not to die
A little.

My Lover Bought Me Saffron

My lover bought me saffron
From a reputable grocer
And in my grinning innocence
I thought it brought us closer,
This meticulous attention
To my culinary needs
With the penises of crocuses
And promises of seeds.

But he has long been absent now
And I am growing sick
Of the limited potential
Of a vegetable dick.
So long has he been missing that
My store is almost gone
And I have used up all the little
Phalluses but one.

I seized it with a tweezers
And upon my palm it lay
With its propagating powder
That my breath could blow away
And I stumbled on a secret
That I never knew I knew;
I closed my eyes and made a wish
And pursed my lips and blew.

I have spiced the space between us
With a cloud of yellow dust
And my lover will be drawn to me
As magic says he must
And I will cook him kedgeree
And memory madras,
With the jissom of a blossom
As a little *coup de grâce.*

I will fill him up with fantasy
As far as I am able
And I will entertain him
From my place across the table
And look into his laughing face
And lose myself among
The golden ghosts of promises
Upon his silver tongue.

"In God's Pocket"

What God's got in his pocket
Nobody really knows,
But I suppose
There's all the usual stuff.
Worldly fluff.
Shiny wrappers-of-things
Twisted to look like wings
Or like trophies in varying sizes
For runners-up prizes.
He'd need a load of those,
God knows.
Tissues – quite a lot –
Soggy tears; crisp snot.
Loose ends of wires and strings
Useful for holding things
Together.
Bright feather
From a bird He's forgotten.
One Smyrna currant (rotten).
Boiled sweet, sucked thin;
Loose change, chucked in.
God's pocket's really deep;
There's room in it for two to sleep.
How about me and you?
That'd do.

No Bad Thing

My heart is giving trouble; it's been battered and abused.
It's not exactly broken but it's definitely bruised.
It should look where it's going but it doesn't, and instead
It clouts itself on corners like a clumsy toddler's head.
It's always doing pratfalls in some private pantomime
And I really can't be doing with it hurting all the time.
I had a try to cry it out but that was not a go –
It just lay there and looked at me pathetically, so
I'll cut it out with scissors and I'll rinse it in a bowl
And mop up any messes with a bit of kitchen roll.
I'll deal with all the dangly bits and wipe off all the froth
And squirt it with deodorant and wrap it in a cloth,
Stick cloves in it and hang it in the wardrobe on a string.
It might dry out and shrivel up, which would be no bad thing.

Forgive me if I don't get up

Pandora speaks

Prometheus was the man that I was made for
But he preferred to join the early martyrs.
He knew I was a prize that would be paid for
And now the gods have had his guts for garters.
I ended up belonging to his brother –
A boring bastard, bless his cotton socks –
He's on some diplomatic trip or other
And I am sitting, knitting, on a box.
Prometheus used to take it into battle
But I have since got rid of all his gear
And now I use it as a sort of settle
To hide the things that I have come to fear.
From time to time all sorts of thoughts have been there.
There's something in it now, as well you know.
It took me all my time to get it in there;
I'm buggered if I'm going to let it go.
I'm a woman of remarkable resilience.
Over the years I've proved that I can cope
With single sorrows that become battalions –
As long as I am not seduced by Hope.
So when again it tempted me to trust it
I moved like shit off the proverbial stick
To whip the rug from under it and thrust it
Into the empty box and shut it quick.
Oh, please! You need me! Let me out! it whinges
But, knowing what would happen if I did,
I've trapped its little fingers in the hinges
And parked my arse securely on the lid.

Pills to Purge Melancholy

And with a green and yellow melancholy
She sat like Patience on a monument
Smiling at grief . . .

Hurrah for homeopathy which posited the notion:
The antidote to everything is in its proper potion.
The cure is in the illness and the answer's in the question;
A little bit of what you ate will fix your indigestion.
Not toe of frog, but hair of dog; a spot of "same again"
And thus the cure for agony is little drips of pain.
There's a simple satisfaction in the logic, but I think
That a melancholy poet needs a literary link.
You could walk into a pharmacy and order "Shit. To go."
The pills are incidental; it is curative to know
That the chemist who concocts them is an educated fellow.
Hurrah for happy Prozac in its coat of green and yellow!

Thinking of you ...

On the 9.30 from Paddington
May 2002

They joined the train at Didcot. Angel faces
On a school trip for pre-pubescent teens.
Bejewelled belly-buttons, dental braces;
All shrunken tops and elephantine jeans.
Now up and down the central aisle strides *Sir*
Seeing his jailbait cargo safely through;
He moves his lips as if in silent prayer,
Counts little titties and divides by two.
Mouthbreathing Tara's adenoidal whine,
Begging to borrow someone's mobile phone,
Descants a giggle-fugue in triple-time
And then it's Bristol Parkway, and they've gone.
If you were here, I'd catch your eye and say –
This Whitsun, I was late getting away ...

Perfect Binding

The poet addresses her lover in a twin-bedded room

Dearest, since we can do no other,
Here on the bed that fate decrees
Let us lie side by side together,
Heads and shoulders, hips and knees
Aligned along a central fissure
Like pages in a paperback;
Conjoined by heat and sticky pressure,
Divided by a constant crack.
And thus, though circumstance divide,
We lie together, if bereft,
Like vellum swelling either side
Of this, our necessary cleft.
So let us live, and let us love,
Proximity is written in
Although we may not always have
The bliss of lying skin to skin.
So let us love, and let us live
As we are simply bound to do;
Our numbers are consecutive,
Our sense and syntax follow through.
If anyone should ever look
We two will be forever found,
Pages in one another's book;
Not stitched, my love, but perfect bound.

Rogue Sunflowers

When the new people moved into our house
They made war on the garden I made you
In the last precious time we had together.
I made it in a season, out of love,
But they destroyed it in an afternoon,
Severing everything above the ground
And tipping the whole lot into a skip.

It was as if it were a colour thing;
They systematically attacked yellow,
Sliced the forsythia off at the waist,
Split it down to the pubic symphysis
And left the rest to die. Slaughtered hypericum;
Cut off the kerria at the stocking-tops,
Leaving its sorry little stumps to bleed.

It was as if they had done this to you;
You were a mender, a lover-better
Of broken things and while you were alive
You hated waste and gracelessness and strife.
At least I could be glad you didn't know;
You couldn't cope with other people's grief
And you would have been ill-at-ease with mine.

I rescued the remains at dead of night,
Digging out stumps, cherishing ravelled roots,
Dragging the earthy burden down the road
To my own house, setting the bits in pots
And ranging them in rows along the wall,
Hoping some of the ruins might survive.
Believing that if they did, so would you.

Birds dropped the seeds. Just like the pantomimes
We saw as children, where, in the nick of time,
They popped out from behind the scenery
And saved lost orphans, so my beggar-birds
Scattered their food over the sleeping plants
And there came sunflowers, sudden, unexpected,
Magnificent and yellow, yellow, yellow.

The Next Best Thing

For Michael Longley

Not Gucci, say the Internet traders,
Casting the word like a sprat on the water;
A lure to tempt the surfing customer
To an experiment with second-best.

A wise man told me that the finest teas
Deserve to be brewed only with snow water.
My water comes down from a mountain, but
It lacks those overtones of sanctity.
Nevertheless, I bless myself with it.

Not snow water, but I make do with it.
My mountain-water comes from underground
And tastes metallic from the long steeping
Of all that colliery waste and dumped slag.
It spurts in fits and starts between two rocks
Beside my kitchen door and dribbles down
Into an artfully assisted puddle.
Frogs shag in it. Occasional small newts
Scuttle across it on their shifty business.
The dog drinks from it; I assume it's safe.

Not snow water, but I make tea with it.
Ty-phoo. Organic. One bag in a mug.
I tell myself it is the next best thing.

The Intrusive Letter

That's what the experts call that special thing
Which, when enunciating certain words,
You do without ever thinking about it,
Casually inserting a rogue sound,
An actual unnecessary letter,
Into a word where no such thing should be;
An unpremeditated naughtiness,
Innocent slip of an unguarded tongue.

Beloved tongue, whose promissory tip
Invisibly spices a public kiss.
Tongue as at home in my mouth as my own.
I know its sweet peculiarities;
I know and love the way it trips a little,
Interposing itself by accident,
Bumping the smooth slide from liquid to sibilant
Confessing to there being someone *eltse.*

Whale Song

Companionship. By mutual consent
They have decided against copulation;
He's still a little pissed, she is content
To have him by osmosis, skin to skin.
A little gentle touching now and then
To keep the options open. It's enough.
They are unquestionably together,
Internal plumbing indistinguishable,
Systems on standby, slowly ticking over,
Their weird harmonics mimicking the song
Of whales whispering across distances
To verify the presence of each other
In the vague wastes of the incurious sea.

The Dream Catchers

Hospital; midnight.

Joseph lies beside Pharaoh's bed on a blanket,
His feet placed carefully between the legs of the drip-stand,
His head alongside the swelling catheter bag.
He is catching the rapid dreams stuttering down to him,
Rapped staccato in time with his master's clenching hands.
His mind works fast, processing the material,
Changing the horror, switching the fantasy
Into good omens and heartening predictions.

Scheherezade is sitting in the corner
Catching the floating facts in the still air,
Combing them slowly between her long, cool fingers,
Dwelling deliberately on small acts of kindness,
Teasing out pleasure from among the pain,
Singing the new songs softly in the night.

I hold a hand of each in each of mine,
Breathing with them, giving their spirits substance,
As they give me their voices in the dark.

Cutting Up His Food

I brought my love a book in hospital.
A great rambling epic of a novel;
A fine tale of tall ships on the high seas
Chosen to tickle a fellow's fantasy,
Tempting him to taste and perhaps consume,
Even if just a little, nourishing
The peaky self that has been lost so long,
Drawing it into daylight on long strings
Of frail imagination.

But it is just too much; too big a portion.
The presentation overfaces him.
Even the meat, though tasty, is not tender;
Tempting, but rather hard to get to grips with.

Here I sit, cutting it up for him
Carefully into manageable pieces.
No problem. This was never gourmet stuff.
Only a bog-standard book club edition.
Flick of a borrowed scalpel – gristly covers
Are consigned to the bin. Skilled filleting
Removes the awkward spine.

I carve it deftly into little penguins,
Labelling each one with a clean, blank page:
Escapist fiction: parts one, two and three.
I bind them carefully, one at a time,
Mending the wounds inflicted on the book
With profligate swathes of the special tape
That binds his own.

Scattering His Ashes

1. Delivery from the "Crem"

The wooden box was passably presented;
It was the bag inside that made me cry.
The stapled see-through plastic I resented,
Although the box was passably presented –
You'd think the wit of man could have invented
Something more suited to a fond goodbye.
The box itself was passably presented.
It was the bag inside that made me cry.

2. Among Roses

I gave you to the roses that you grew
Because I knew you would be happy there.
Now you are part of what was part of you.

Because you used to love to look into
The face of *Madame Alfred Carrière,*
I gave you to the roses that you grew.

Zéphirine Drouhin will be nourished through
The goodness of the man who thought her fair,
Now you are part of what was part of you.

To let you stroke a *Cuisse de Nymphe émue,*
Her blushing cheek, her saucy derrière,
I gave you to the roses that you grew

And when it rains I hear you talking to
Sturdy *Penelope* in the parterre,
Now you are part of what was part of you.

See mighty *Kiftsgate,* lusty parvenu,
Hoisting you thirty feet into the air!
I gave you to the roses that you grew;
Now you are part of what was part of you.

3. Launched off the Coast of Crete.

Now, my Odysseus, I will send you home
To Ithaca. You would have approved of that.

First I must leave you sitting on a rock,
Safe in the pocket of my dressing gown,
While I pick my way over stuttering shingle
To make an arrangement with Poseidon.
Setting myself afloat in the shallows
I lie a long time, letting the water shift me,
My belly rubbing on the weedy stones
Like a spawned-out kelt.

Arising – *Venus Anadyomene* –
Salt water dribbling from my hefty thighs,
I note the appearance of the ocean.
A rumpled tablecloth, wine-stains and all;
No tide, no pull, no undercurrent.
Wishing a wind to help you find the way,
I take you, in your plastic screw-top boat,
And fling you, straight from the shoulder, out, out
In the wrong direction, trusting to the good offices
Of the accommodating sea.

4. Poohsticks in Paris

You never did take me to Paris, sweetheart,
I brought you here instead. I smuggled you
Through customs, disguised as a roll of film.
Today I carried you in my red handbag
Across the Pont-au-Double to Nôtre Dame.

It was as though they had known we were coming.
Baroque music was flowing from the doors.
I thought of God, squatting somewhere inside
Engaged in Creative Visualisation –
You used to do that, love, do you remember?
With Albinoni, candles and a hassock?

Whatever made me think you'd be at home
In a cathedral? You'd prefer the river –

Poohsticks! From the upstream side of the bridge
I lobbed you out onto the heaving bosom
Of the scurrying Seine. She caught you deftly,
Held you and ran with you under my feet.
I tried to cross, to see you tumble through,
But the road was full of the mad traffic
We would imagine when we played at Paris –
Ah, Monsieur Farquinelle! Où est la plume
De vôtre tante sacrée. Non! Merde, alors . . .

I made it. Just. The tiny white container
Whizzed like a sprinter down the wide brown lane.
I cheered you out of sight – *Go, lover, go!*

5. Remembering Proust

You used to tell me that Proust was buried
In Jews Wood Cemetery, Newport, Gwent.
Although I knew it was one of your wind-ups
Like the mythical town of Dickhead, Minnesota
I always secretly hoped it was true.

But I have found him now, in *Père Lachaise*
Irretrievably immured in black marble.
I have dibbled a hole in the gravel
Next to his tomb with a Swiss army knife
And carefully peppered a drift of ashes
Onto the slightly sour earth underneath.

Combing the small stones gently over you
With grubby fingers, I am celebrating
A fitting end to our *folie à deux*
And a fine way to win an argument.

6. Feeding the Ducks at Calstock

This was one of the places we had shared.
I had imagined I would be alone;
The place was packed with grockles. I was scared
To make much ceremony on my own.
The smell of chips lay heavy on the air,
The day was hot, the Tamar brown and thick.
I needed to complete my business there
And felt it would be best if I were quick:
Off with the lid, a surreptitious fling.
A cloud of spinning bits sank in the murk
And, terrified of missing anything,
All the assembled wildfowl went berserk.
Feeding the ducks? I heard somebody say.
Something like that, I said, and turned away.

7. *Plodging at Whitley Bay*

The beach is deserted. I'll empty your tin
At the edge of the ocean. The tide's coming in
And the water will take you and make you a part
Of its practical purpose, its innocent art.
In the language of limestone it solemnly sings
Of corals and cliffs and ephemeral things.

Now the foam is encroaching as if it's aware of
The thing it's been given to love and take care of.
It curtseys and bobs with a coy little hiss
Then purses its lips in a whiskery kiss.
The flocculent fag-ash is eager to fly
But the little white hard bits refuse to comply.

So forward and back go the brisk little waters,
The sifters and winnowers, sharers and sorters
And when it is over the thing is decided,
You are played-for and won; you are lost and divided.
You are part of the ocean and part of the land;
Dispersed in the sea and ensconced in the sand.

8. *The Amphitheatre at Caerleon*

Appropriate? I thought so. We were both
Enthralled by Rome. You were a businessman,
I was a farmer. We were both concerned
With thoughts of empire and responsibility.
This brought you, at the end, to study here:
Romano-Celtic archaeology.

You fell half way to your Master's degree
Like a defeated gladiator. *Requies.*

And here was where I found the broken sign –
This way to the Roman Baths; white on brown
As is deemed meet for ancient monuments.
It had been snapped off where it joined the post.
I found it hidden in some little bushes
And asked the warden if he wanted it:

No, you can have it, love. It can't be mended.
It's cast you see, that means you can't weld it.
All you can do is make another one.
If you can find the mould. And if there's time…

Winter Camping

One thing was always understood between us.
When you were ready to go Winter Camping
I would not be a part of the adventure.

You bought equipment and wrote plans in journals,
Calling it Personal Development,
Anticipating solitude and challenge.

You never did it. Life got in the way
Until death stopped the prospect altogether.
I have not often thought about it since.

Sleeping without you was a big adventure.
A single bed, electrically warmed,
Beside the open door onto the balcony.

Birds visited. Various gastropods
Slid over the threshold and were welcome.
Cats came and went. Last night there was a storm.

I went to sleep enchanted by the wind.
It died in the small hours; the silence woke me.
I am in an extraordinary place.

Dark, starred with tiny lights across the valley,
Clouded with frozen breath. I move carefully,
Explore the limits of my warm cocoon.

Now on my left there is a precipice.
Cold fingers trace the edges of my ears.
I am alone and this is Winter Camping.

Matinée

The lights go up to much polite applause.
Crocodile bags snap up discarded glasses
With the finality of a firing squad.
Heads rise and fall, like pianola keys
In shades of grey. Opinions trickle out
Discreetly, as the sitters and their seats
Resume, one at a time, an upright posture.

A certain redolence hangs in the air,
There and not-there. Matinée-goers' must.
A whiff of crotch, a polyester squeak;
The faintest taint of armpit as good coats,
Not worn for everyday, are flipped about
And shrugged-on, to equip the regiment
Against the rearguard of the afternoon.

Three Plays, Four Quartets and Five People You Meet in Heaven...

Visiting an Internet bookshop. For Sebastian.

I let myself in, quiet as a thief, with my own key.
In the Emporium I unpack my bag of silence,
Set up my echoes either side of myself
Like speakers, carefully adjusting woof and tweet
So as to make my own voice lovely, even out my breathing
Into a pleasing meditative wheeze.
Here's where I come to find my own lost past;
Here at my elbow, in a cup of English Breakfast
I dip digestives with consummate skill
Born of long practice. I am alone with books.
I'm real and they are real. Only the place is fake.
No sweet smell of degenerating paper,
None of the holy feel of the real thing,
But I have spliced in the odd grunt of high reaching
And the creak of imaginary floorboards.
Here's where I come to drink mandragora
When the damp of hell is making my bones ache,
My own voice irks me and I think of ways
To edit out the breathing altogether.

Remaindered

One day I'll have the heart to joke about it –
"Arrival of the Book Box!" – *ha-ha-ha!*
But now it squats like Giant Disappointment
Between the front door and the bottom stair.

On one side of the cube, right in the middle
A plastic envelope has been stuck on.
I dare not take the letter from the wrapper
Because the burden of it is "Dear John ... "

I know I am confusing oeuvre and ego
And that each from the other is removed
But down among the polystyrene kidneys
A little of the author lies unloved.

If I were Shelley I would turn to crystal
The pure transcendence of poetic pain.
If I were Sophocles I'd blame Olympus.
If I were Maupassant I'd go insane.

If I were Barbara Pym I'd write to Larkin
But that's no good to me because he's dead.
I can't feel any fellowship with Belloc;
His sins were scarlet – but his books were read!

If I were Hardy I'd contrive a novel
Of hope doomed to dissolve into despair.
Corneille would have embellished it with thunder:
Ah, Boîte! dont la vue seule me jette envers l'enfer!

But now, poor cow, I've not the heart to shift it;
All I can do is sit on it and blub.
I am Oor Wullie on his upturned bucket:
Whit'll ah dae? – Jings! Crivvens! Help ma Boab!

Slightly Foxed

For Harper Levine, antiquarian bookseller.

New: Unexpectedly available.
Offered by an anonymous collector.
With interesting cryptic dedication.
A privately-commissioned gift edition
Of this sought-after author. Seldom seen.
Still in original wrap-round jacket.
No major faults apparent.   Good for age.
Slight crinkling. Evidence of wear to spine.
A little faded, with a few small tears.
Otherwise fine.

Stuff . . .

Is the proverbial bag of rocks we carry
Until we are ready to set them down.
Some of them really are rocks, like as not.

Pieces of beaches. One with an impressed fern.
One with a little face that grinned among
The amazing grapeshot of the south coast.

Old toys, conflating loving and possession.
Items and things. Memorabilia
Kept to give us a handle on forever.

Themed collections, arising from shared passions.
Parting gets harder, and the fear of loss
Heightens the urgency of acquisition.

Stuff narrows vision, accretes in the corners
Of eyes whose lids cannot blink it away.
It blocks the ducts, impedes the flow of tears,

That's what it's for. Keepsakes, remembrances.
Fossil remains of things already lost
That we are never ready to betray.

And so we die beneath the weight of it,
Persisting in heretical belief
In the holiness of accumulation;

A sort of martyrdom, pressed to death under
The precious evidence of lost mythologies,
The unbearable poignancy of stuff.

The Case for Light Verse

For John Whitworth

Beside the epic, with its long tradition
Of mythic reference and erudition,
Darling of bards po-faced and reverential,
Light verse seems horribly inconsequential.
There is no literary substance to it,
No lasting value; any fool can do it.
Take up the burden that distorts your soul,
Crack it and tip it out into a bowl;
Discard the yolk and then with merry vigour
Whip up the white and add a bit of sugar.
This is a recipe that can't go wrong;
A little biscuit melting on the tongue,
Tickling the idiot's fancy like a feather
Making him laugh and clamour for another.
No one expects us amiable asses
To seek to reach the peak of Mount Parnassus,
Therefore, dear heart, let us write fast and louche
And give the common man his *amuse-bouche*.
Write light. Let rip with a poetic fart.
That way they may conclude we have no heart
But those who really matter will know better.

The Dover Bitch Criticises Her Life

After Hecht, after Arnold

I am waiting on the beach.   Soon the car door will slam,
Then shingle will mutter grudgingly under his feet.
He will come. He will keep the old promise. I will not turn
                                                    round.
We'll meet with the light behind me; a year is a long time.
Here's where we first met, in the far-off days
When I was a poet's muse.   How he laughed at me then;
Laughed till we fell serious, fell accidentally into bed,
Since when, again and again we have fallen together,
Though the fallings are growing further and further apart . . .
This is how it will be. A kiss.   A meal somewhere decent.
A wine from across the water, for old times' sake.
And afterwards, tipsy and sad, I will treat him right.
I will treat him to all the year's longing in one great lay.
I will nurse him asleep on breasts that are not what they were;
Try not to consider the different levels of love.
Oh, my beloved, insensitive, cynical swine;
I want him here, sharing old jokes and taking the piss
Out of my 'O' Level Greek. A year is a long time
But I am still Persephone, albeit gone to seed;
Six months remembering, then six anticipating.
Heaven knows, I was never a greedy woman
But I hope he remembers the bottle of *Nuit d'Amour*.
I'm almost out. And that's what gets me through
Between times. The merest whiff on a tissue
Shushes the fears, tempers the imaginings,
Taking the raw edge off the gnawing knowing
That my long loss is someone else's gain.

The Fat White Woman Considers Her Options

Where did it all go, all the rest of it?
Guess there must have been a hole in
Mama's brand new bag.

Shit. I can see right down into the bottom;
Looks like there isn't a great deal of anything
Left in it at all.

Oh, what can I do with the disappearing dregs of it?
Build a big hutch and keep fancy rabbits
So I can still stroke hair?

Or a dog, to snuffle and twitch and dream visibly
And ensure I could still sniff up the occasional fart
That was not my own.

Should I chuck the dumb fluff and fill the bag with rubble;
Carry it high on my shoulder so it feels
Like a sleeping head?

Or sit here sad on what's left of it, considering options
Till I howl till it hurts like hell, or at least
Till I piss myself laughing

And I can say to the postman and the gasman –
Brutha, yu can kiss mi big fat ass
Cos hey! de world mi oyster
An no man jacka yu gonna kiss dat.

Traditional Seaside Fun

Peter is here. See how he stares, engrossed,
into the kingdom of the captive crane.
The single article he covets most
has pulled him down the pier to try again.
At last the mouth-organ is standing proud
of all the other treasures in the cage;
he drops the maximum he is allowed
into the slot and feels the wheels engage.
Slowly the boom swings out above the prize –
this time he has it! Metal fingers shut
securely round the instrument. He tries
to reel it in, almost succeeding, but
a relaxation that he can't prevent
causes the grapple to relinquish it
and swing back empty and incompetent
to dangle sullenly above the pit
before spreading its faithless fingers wide
to drop sod all into his waiting hand.
He couldn't win however hard he tried
but Peter, gutted, doesn't understand.

Simon is here too, poised to make his bid.
Peter's face falls, Simon's right arm swings in
to overhang the disappointed kid;
Hard luck, young man! – he dons a rueful grin –
I really thought you had that cut and dried.
I'd be pissed off if it did that to me.
But I think I've got one of those inside
that I could give you. Shall we go and see?
His fingers close round Peter's upper arm
so very gently you would hardly know.
Young Peter has no inkling of alarm,
but Simon isn't going to let go.

Peter still turns up almost every day,
taking for granted Simon's being here;
he's never short of what it takes to play
the many games that flourish on the pier.
His tongue between his teeth, he tries again.
Bearing in mind all that he has been told,
he fixes his attention on the crane;
targets the watch that looks as though it's gold.

The Culture Secretary has decided that, although children are banned from playing arcade games that cost more than 10 pence, an exception should be made in the case of the mechanical crane, which costs 30p but is classified as "traditional seaside fun".

Unicorn

I was a kid again, swinging thin legs
That didn't reach the floor, imagining
The unicorn she asked me to create
Out of my head, seeing it come alive.

This was my first attempt at such a thing.
Without putting too fine a point on it,
You only get one shot at unicorns.
You catch them at the cost of innocence.

And oh, I caught the beauty bang to rights!
I nailed his hooves as they clicked on the flags
I snatched and held the ripples of his rump
And fixed his gentle gaze on the blank page.

I rolled out the long horn between my hands;
I spun his mane out of new-minted words;
I curled my fingers in the silver ringlets
And brought him smugly to my lady's feet.

Thank you, said she. *Now I will show you something*
That will amaze you. You thought you had written
A unicorn. But it's a "metaphor" –
And I will use it for a waterfall.

Only an adult could betray a child
So absolutely. I had given her
The thing I thought she wanted; now it seemed
That all along she wanted something else.

She only had to ask; I would have written
A waterfall that would have swept her heart
Straight into Paradise. She could have said.
But no. She had to kill the unicorn.

She broke his ears off, stuck them either side
Of her own creation. Took his living mane
And trickled it across the shining rocks
That used to be his feet. I wept for him.

I made this poem from the broken bits
I have kept hidden under the waterfall
For all these years. Take it; it is for you.
A second-hand, recycled unicorn.

Mad Annie Explains All

*For those people who make assumptions about the bunch of babies'
dummies that hangs by my front door.*

In the house of the hanging noonoos
At the sign of the surrogate tit,
In mysterious mess lived an anchoress
Who collected discarded kit.

At the house of the dangling didies
She created an installation
That turned each find of the comforter kind
To a source of inspiration

Till her cherished collection of cushies
Became a delightful distraction
Whenever she thought in more depth than she ought
About oral satisfaction

And under the tumbling numnums
She would sit by herself and sigh
At the pitiful waste that her lapse of good taste
Exposed to the public eye.

For they sell them in packets of seven
As an easy commitment to bliss,
A knee-jerk reaction to dissatisfaction,
An over-the-counter kiss

And each of the colourful dumdums,
As far as she could discover,
Had slipped from the grip of an infant lip
Like a taken-for-granted lover

And if anyone noticed its downfall
It was always discreetly ignored
Till the madwoman came and pocketed same
To add to her magical hoard.

Now she sits by herself in her hovel
With the relics that should have been binned
And the noonoos, the numnums, the little kiss-condoms
Revolve in the winnowing wind.

The Baby's Hat

Some closet paedophile must have devised
This tortured pseudo-medieval shape,
Where two gross knitted twists rise either side
Of the bizarrely gift-wrapped fontanelle
To hang erratically at sad angles –
The shattered horns of a Levantine goat
Defeated in the rut. A feeble thread
Of ersatz swansdown burrows in and out
Of a row of ill-crafted openwork,
Emerging in apologetic tufts
Above the ears, like unsuccessful ferrets
Sniffing the wind, seeking the best way home.
Pink nylon ribbon mingles with the fluff
To form a background for the masterstroke –
Fat plastic pearls, clinging like beads of sweat
Around the baby's flaky little forehead,
Artfully mirroring the beads of snot
Collected in its nostrils. I am moved
To snatch the child, to run away with it,
To hold it somewhere safe while I contrive
To conjure up a less abusive hat.

Prima Donna

All dressed in pink, indubitably blonde,
White socks and patent shoes. Someone's princess
Is far from happy, judging by the sobbing.
Squeezing her eyes so as to make juice ooze
Between wet lashes. Slumping to the ground
In a collapse of grief. But not for loss;
She weeps for something she would rather like
And thinks she may not get. Ah, Brava! Brava!

> *Arding and Hobbs in nineteen forty-seven.*
> *What little cash changed hands was spirited*
> *Along taut wires, singing overhead*
> *Like angels, sacred, unattainable.*

The mousy little girl in hand-me-downs
With droopy hem and pudding-basin hair
Watches the performance, dispassionate.
Her mother takes her hand and holds it tight.
"Look at that naughty little girl" she says.
That's not the way to get the things you want,
Is it? People who sulk and whinge for things
Are disappointed. It's good girls like you,
Patient and understanding, who will get
Everything in the end. Her daughter smiles.

> *Comforting thought: "some day my prince will come".*
> *An easy, inexpensive opiate*
> *In those days of postwar austerity.*
> *Snake-oil and bullshit; close your eyes and swallow.*

The little girl in pink is gathered up
And comforted. Attendants brush her down
And dry her tears. Bring her a severed head
On a Bunnykins dish.

With Ron

I have come with Ron to the hospital
Where experts hope to help his crippled frame
Stand up a little longer. Diabetes
Sucks at his eyes and nibbles at his toes.
We sit and wait until they call his name.

He had it hard, did Ron, when he was little.
The Lord gave him poliomyelitis
And stuck a cosmic swozzle in his throat
So that he speaks in squawks. I am condemned
To listen to his braying conversation,
See-saw South-Walian reiteration
Of each remark. Phatic regurgitation
Of tabloid pseudo-news. I have a book
But cannot read it. That would be unkind.

And I believe in kindness. I help Ron
Because he needs someone. I volunteered.
At first I coasted it; did easy things
That cost me nothing. Letter to the "Social" –
Creative Writer in her element.
Now his old Mam glides up and down the stairs
On a free lift and gets into the bath
All by herself. I made them hurry up
With his new boots. Look – he is wearing them.

Oh, how good you are to the poor old sod,
Say the approving faces. But I see it
More as a trade-off with the Almighty.
I live alone, agreeably immersed
In my own world of self-preoccupation.
But on the day it comes – as come it will,
The Diagnosis or the Accident –
If for some reason I can't reach the switch,
I will have need of the kindness of others.

Nominal Aphasia

My words are not my servants any more;
They did not answer me when called upon:
I wanted dynamo; they gave me Thermidor

At first I found it funny – "*merde alors!* –
Where did that naughty little thought come from?
My words are not my servants any more!"

I smiled and went on trying; I was sure
The simple hitch could quickly be undone.
I fished for dynamo and landed Thermidor.

I called the thralls who always helped before
But all their old obedience was gone,
My words were not my servants any more.

I felt the terror then, the groping for
The thing that used to make the light come on.
If I need dynamo, what use is Thermidor?

It's like the quiet closing of a door,
The crossing of a private Rubicon.
My words are not my servants any more.
I wanted dynamo; they gave me Thermidor.

Repetitive Strain Injury

On diagnosis I gave way to grief,
fearing my writing life was at an end.
*It hurts to do the thing that brings relief
from all the other pain,* I told a friend.
Mischievously misunderstanding me,
he said, *get a vibrator; that'll do it,*
and I, amused by his audacity,
decided there might be some substance to it.
I can recall first finding language fun
and being fascinated to discover
that substituting letters one by one
could change a given word into another.
Writing soon turns to self-abuse indeed;
Waiting and *Wanting* are the steps you need.

The Word Made Flesh

For Tony Rowe

On the broad steps of the cathedral
The feckless hopefully hold out their hands,
Often with some success; the privileged
Lighten their consciences by a few pence
On their way to receive the sacrament.

On the seventeenth step two beggars sit
Paying no regard to the worshippers
Who file past on their way to salvation.
They do not ask for alms. They are engrossed;
Skilfully masturbating one another.

Most who have noticed this pretend they haven't;
Some of the other beggars wish they wouldn't.
Poor relief is incumbent on the rich
And by taking things into their own hands
They spoil the scene for everybody else.

Our Lord said, "silver and gold have I none
But such as I have give I thee". The words
Are here made flesh; with beatific sigh
One gives the other benison, slipping
All that he has into the waiting hand
Of somebody who shares his human need.

The newly shriven filter down the steps
Averting their eyes from the seventeenth,
Where the first beggar, in a state of grace,
Works selflessly towards the second coming.

Nuns, Skating

Nuns fret not at their convent's narrow room
Because their spirits can escape beyond
The place that holds them in respectful gloom
To seek the Lord beside the frozen pond.
There He will make their laughter into bells
And turn their breath to incense. He will show
Shadows of magi on the distant hills
And flights of angels shining in the snow.
He will make rushes sing and grasses dance
To the intrusive music of their chatter,
Whispering in their ears that, just this once,
They too can walk as He did, on the water.
Oh, may the year to come be full of these
Small serendipitous epiphanies.

Written in a Christmas card with the picture "Winter at the Convent"
by Margaret Loxton

For Larry – The Sonnet I Promised

i.m. L.K.McElroy

Sad is too small a word; it will not do.
It cannot carry what is in my heart.
I want to say the right goodbye to you;
The tricky bit is knowing where to start.
Grief is too big somehow, and not your style;
You couldn't do with that pretentious shit,
Always preferring what would make you smile.
You wouldn't wear it if it didn't fit.
It's out there somewhere in the sudden dark –
The slick one-liner that will say it all –
And when I find it I will bring it back
And spray it scarlet on a public wall.
Poetry sucks. This is real McCoy:
I'm gonna miss you, Mr. McElroy

Meeting Apollo

In the Barbara Hepworth Sculpture Garden

Snide giggle of soft rain on foliage
As I recognised him in the garden.
Tenth figure among the damp shrubs. Apollo.
I shed tears in exchange for his wet blessing,
Apotheosis of a naughty whim.

There was a tangle of steel reinforcement
Beckoning from a lump of broken concrete
That somebody had chucked into a skip;
A lucky find, a nice bit of rough trade
Calling out, asking to be taken home.

Compassion for the beauty in found things
Gave me the right to take it; now it lives
Lovely in long grass in my own garden,
Moss on its plinth, rust on the twisted rods
That mimic the perfection of Apollo.

That's how I live, occasionally blessed
By random glimpses of the sad old god
Who wanders through the wreckage of the world
Twanging the slack strings of a busted lyre,
Seeking an echo in a mortal heart.